Set design by Max DeArmon

A scene from the New York production of *In Arabia We'd All Be Kings*.

Photo by Sarah Sidman

IN ARABIA WE'D
ALL BE KINGS

BY STEPHEN ADLY GUIRGIS

DRAMATISTS
PLAY SERVICE
INC.

IN ARABIA WE'D ALL BE KINGS
Copyright © 2002, Stephen Adly Guirgis

All Rights Reserved

SPECIAL NOTE

SPECIAL NOTE ON SONGS AND RECORDINGS

IN ARABIA WE'D ALL BE KINGS was first presented by LAByrinth Theater Company at CenterStage (Philip Seymour Hoffman and John Ortiz, Artistic Directors) in New York City on June 23, 1999. It was directed by Philip Seymour Hoffman; the set design was by Max DeArmon; the lighting design was by Sarah Sidman; the sound design was by Eric DeArmon; the costume design was by Mimi O'Donnell; and the production stage manager was Doreen Feldman. The cast was as follows:

LENNY	David Zayas
SKANK	Trevor Long
DAISY	Liza Colon Zayas
SAMMY	Mark Hammer
DEMARIS	Ana Ortiz
MISS REYES	Begonya Plaza
JAKE	Richard Petrocelli
VIC/CARROLL/MAN #1	Felix Solis
CHARLIE	Salvatore Inzerillo
CHICKIE	Tiprin Mandalay
GREER/RAKIM	Russell G. Jones
HOLY ROLLER/MAN #2/SAL	Chris McGarry

CHARACTERS

LENNY

SKANK

DAISY

SAMMY

DEMARIS

MISS REYES

JAKE

VIC/CARROLL/MAN #1

CHARLIE

CHICKIE

GREER/RAKIM

HOLY ROLLER/MAN #2/SAL

PLACE

New York City.

TIME

Present.

IN ARABIA WE'D ALL BE KINGS

ACT ONE

Scene 1

Monday, three o'clock A.M. The bar.

LENNY. *(To Skank.)* There's two kinds a peoples in this world: those who annoy the shit outta me, but not enough for me to actually beat them; and those that are so fuckin' annoying that even after I beat them, I still don' feel no satisfaction 'cuz I can still feel them inside a me, like when you eat some bad shit, like some crazy Indian food, and it just stays in there! You can't even shit it out 'cuz it, it lingers! You hear what I'm sayin': Linger!

DAISY. I want my money, Lenny!

LENNY. *(To Skank.)* Put it this way: If I was the Mayor, I'd make a law that stated that all people such as yourself, if you kill them, all you get is like a summons!

SKANK. Listen, man —

LENNY. — One more thing: Get your hand out the peanuts!

SKANK. Hey, big guy man, I have a right —

LENNY. — You have a right?! You have no rights. I'm a put it like this —

DAISY. Lenny —

LENNY. *(To Daisy.)* Stick a clam in it!

DAISY. You stick a clam in it!

5

LENNY. I should stick a clam in it?! Lemme tell you this — *(To Skank.)* Hey! You think I'm playin'? Eat a peanut! Go ahead, eat a peanut! Please eat a peanut with those filthy hands so I could decapitate them right off your wrists like a lawn mower. I'll go "Whaa-chump!" you'll be handless!

DAISY. Lenny —

LENNY. And you too! I'll "Whaa-chump" you, you'll be lipless! You'll be talkin shit, people be saying, "What Daisy talkin' about?" and they'll be like, "I don' know, bitch ain't got no lips!"

DAISY. Gimme my money, Lenny!

LENNY. Money? Whatchyoo talkin', money? *(To Skank.)* Where you going?

SKANK. Jukebox.

LENNY. I'll allow you to play A7, E4, and *(To Daisy.)* Baby, what's that other one I like by that rock guy wit' the —

DAISY. Gimme my money!

LENNY. *(To Skank.)* A7, E4, you play anything I don' like, I'll beat you.

SKANK. Okay.

DAISY. Lenny —

LENNY. *(To Skank.)* And wipe down the buttons after you press them. *(To Daisy.)* He prolly got the herps, right baby? *(Shouts.)* Where's the beer taker? Yo beer! … *(To himself.)* Irish motherfuck-ahs, they're either standing over you like vultures waiting for you to fuck up, or they're disapearin to the bathroom like cyphers: *(To Daisy.)* Did he bring the paper with him?

SKANK. … Uh … dude? You got any, like, a coupla quarters?

LENNY. What??!!

SKANK. It's juss that … Nevermind. *(Skank goes to jukebox.)*

LENNY. Goddamn right, "Nevermind"! This ain't no Banco Popular, mothahfuckah! *(To Daisy.)* Man thinks I'm a ATM! *(To Skank.)* I ain't no ATM!

DAISY. I coulda told him that.

LENNY. What chu mean by that?

DAISY. Lissen —

LENNY. What chu tryin to instigate? Huh?

DAISY. You need to check yourself, Lenny.

LENNY. I need to check myself?

DAISY. You need to check your ass.

LENNY. Check my ass?

DAISY. Don't talk to me.

LENNY. You need to check your ass! You better check your ass, or your ass'll be checked for you!

DAISY. Please.

LENNY. You'll be checking your ass into St. Claire's after I beat that ass, with your lip talkin to me like that.

DAISY. You wanna try me?

LENNY. I'm the man. You not the man. I'm the man. Respect the man.

DAISY. Respect the man.

LENNY. Dass right. "Respect the man, you respect yourself."

DAISY. Don't talk that jail talk.

LENNY. Respect the man!

DAISY. You still locked up?

LENNY. Respect the man.

DAISY. Respect the man?

LENNY. Juss like that.

DAISY. "Respect the man."

LENNY. End of story.

DAISY. Respect the fat, unemployed, lives wit' his momma, man.

LENNY. You're crossing the border, baby.

DAISY. Why don' you cross the border, get your ass a job, stop leechin'.

LENNY. You know what a leech is? A leech is a vermin. Point blank: You think I'm a species of vermin?

DAISY. I'm going to the Chinese —

LENNY. — How you going to Chinese without me?

DAISY. One time! Gimme my money or I'll call your P.O. right now, "Lenny's in a bar, he hit me, he got the crack in his pocket."

LENNY. Call him!

DAISY. Fine.

LENNY. Wait! ... C'mon, Let's go Chinese together, be friends.

DAISY. I don' think you wanna test me.

LENNY. I'm hungry.

DAISY. Lenny!

LENNY. Okay, okay. Here take the money, bring me back a

7

Kung Foo Platter, some ribs, coupla spring rolls —

DAISY. Later for you.

LENNY. Yo, what kinda welcome home is this?

DAISY. Welcome home? I been Welcoming your crusty ass home all week. You been welcomed. You want some more welcoming?

LENNY. I'm juss sayin —

DAISY. You are welcome to buy your own cigarettes. You are welcome to pay for your own drinks —

LENNY. — You got a short memory 'cuz —

DAISY. You are welcome to buy the fuckin' paper and look for a damn job!

LENNY. Fine! Fine! You wanna steak dinner? C'mon, less go. I'm gonna buy you a steak dinner with a bottle a wine and a friggin' pecan pie with the pistachio ice cream. C'mon, less go.

DAISY. You ain't buyin' shit.

LENNY. I'll buy it. Whaddya want? A yacht? 'Cuz I'll buy you a yacht. You know why? 'Cuz I love you —

DAISY. PSSSsssssss!

LENNY. Don' you walk away from me! Hey! ...

DAISY. What? *(Pause.)*

LENNY. Save me a coupla chicken wings. *(Daisy turns away, goes to exit.)* I'll see you when you come back ... *(She exits.)* Daisy! ... Heartless! She a heartless individual ... Sammy! ... Sammy, your wife fuck wit' you like dat?

SAMMY. My wife?

LENNY. Yeah.

SAMMY. She here?

LENNY. Nah, Sam.

SAMMY. Good.

LENNY. Gladdis fucks with you?

SAMMY. Gladdis?

LENNY. Your wife!

SAMMY. My wife? ... You mean Gladdis?

LENNY. Yeah. She fucks with you, right?

SAMMY. Fifty years.

LENNY. Long time.

SAMMY. Fifty-one years next month.

LENNY. But you love her, right? ... Sammy? ... Sammy?

SAMMY. Huh?

LENNY. You love your wife?

SAMMY. My wife?

LENNY. Yeah.

SAMMY. My wife? ... Fuck my wife!

LENNY. Okay. *(Pause.)*

SAMMY. She here?

LENNY. No, Sammy.

SAMMY. Good. Fuck her.

LENNY. Fuck Daisy too! Fuck them all, except my mother. Sammy, you know my mother, right?

SAMMY. Fuck your mother!

LENNY. Sammy, take it easy ... I'm talkin about my moms. You know my moms, she come in sometimes, Marisol. You know Marisol, right Sammy? Sammy?

SAMMY. Marisol?

LENNY. Dass right.

SAMMY. I like Marisol.

LENNY. Thank you.

SAMMY. Everybody likes Marisol.

LENNY. Did she ever make you her pernil?

SAMMY. Marisol, she's good. I like Marisol.

LENNY. She raised me.

SAMMY. I'll tell ya somethin' ... My wife here?

LENNY. Nah, Sammy.

SAMMY. Good. I used to know a Puerto Rican lady named Marisol, back when I was still drivin' the bus.

LENNY. Yeah?

SAMMY. She had a big ass!

LENNY. Yeah?

SAMMY. I like that.

LENNY. Right.

SAMMY. Gladdis ... Is she here?

LENNY. No, Sam.

SAMMY. Gladdis got no ass to speak of. She got that Irish ass, looks like a saltine cracker.

LENNY. She gotta flat ass?

SAMMY. Gladdis' ass and my ass, it's the same ass, exact same,

9

but this lady, the senorita Marisol, she had a big ass.

LENNY. Uh huh.

SAMMY. I like that. *(Pause.)*

LENNY. Yeah. The thing wit' Daisy, is, like, she say, "Why you live wit' your moms," you know, like chumpin' me and shit, and I'm supposed ta juss take her abuse, 'cuz thass the word for it, it's fuckin abuse. But what I would like ta say to her, but I can't 'cuz then it'd be like World War Three, is, "You live wit' my mothah too, bitch! At least I got a mothah to live wit'! You think I need you constantly reminding me that I'm past thirty-five still livin' at home?" ... Thing is Sammy, like, maybe you could ... Sammy? ... Sammy?

SAMMY. I ate a banana in 1969, thought it was an avocado.

LENNY. Sam?

SAMMY. Avocado ...

LENNY. Sammy? *(Skank returns from jukebox.)*

SKANK. Um, Lenny?

LENNY. Stop it. *(To Sam.)* Sammy? ... *(To himself.)* Drunks ... Useless ...

SKANK. Lenny —

LENNY. *(To Skank.)* You still here? Beat it.

SKANK. Listen, a, Lenny —

LENNY. Don't call me by my name, that's my name! I get called by my name from those I choose to allow them the privilege. Get outta here! Now!

SKANK. I juss thought maybe you could pick the songs you like, man, because, a, A7 and E4, there's nothing there, and so, why don't you just pick the songs?

LENNY. I should pick the songs?

SKANK. Yeah.

LENNY. I look like a DJ?

SKANK. I don't know, but, I got some selections over there, paid for, and, uh, maybe, I mean if you want, you could play E12 'cuz a, fuck, did I say E12? I meant B12, it's a, dag, what is her name? You know, she was a jazz singer, she was a junkie? Dag, man, it's on the tip a my —

LENNY. Get the fuck out outta here now!

SKANK. You know what? We don't have to listen to music 'cuz,

10

a, music … music, fuck music! Right? Fuckin' music fuckin' sucks!

LENNY. Wass your name?

SKANK. My name?

LENNY. You know what? I don't need to know your name, I'm gonna give you a name. Your name is "About to Get Your Ass Kicked Fuckin' Skank." You got that?

SKANK. Hey man, that's … I don't like that.

LENNY. You don't like that?

SKANK. I mean, it's cool, I guess, but —

LENNY. Listen, Skank, it's time for you to go.

SKANK. Okay, okay, I'll just be quiet, okay?

LENNY. No.

SKANK. I'll sit in the back.

LENNY. No.

SKANK. See, man, the thing is, thing is I got a drink coming, from the guy, the bartender, so, a, I'd like to just —

LENNY. Do you see a bartender?

SKANK. Do I see a, no, but …

LENNY. Do you see this knife?

SKANK. Okay. I'm leaving. *(Skank exits. A beat. He returns.)* This is wrong, man, this is, I want my drink! My drink is owed to me and I want it, and if you wanna fuckin stab me, than fuckin stab! Okay? I been stabbed before, I'll be stabbed again, fuck it man, stab! *(Lenny goes to stab him.)* Whoa! Whoa! Wait! I'm goin', I'm goin! *(Skank exits again. A beat. Skank opens the door very slightly and whispers through the crack.)* Dude? Big guy? Whoa, Whoa! Don't get up. Listen. I'm gonna wait out here. When the bartender comes back, I'm gonna get my buy back, guzzle it, and split. Okay? Okay? … Right, great, I'll be out here. *(Skank exits, a pause, the bar door opens.)*

LENNY. That's it, death! *(Miss Reyes and DeMaris enter.)* Oh. Hi, Miss Reyes. Hi, DeMaris.

MISS REYES. Oh my God! When you got out, baby?!

DEMARIS. It's fuckin' pourin' out there.

MISS REYES. Guttermouth!

DEMARIS. Chicken Head!

MISS REYES. If you want to drink on my check, you better reconsider that attitude.

DEMARIS. My hair's all fucked up!

MISS REYES. Keep playin' games wit' me, see what happens. *(To Lenny.)* Whassamatter, Poppo, no hugs and kisses? Don' be stingy, baby, give it up. *(They embrace, Lenny halfheartedly, Miss Reyes with gusto.)*

MISS REYES. Mira, Lenny, you lookin' good, Poppo. They feeded you good up there, eh?

DEMARIS. How come Daisy at the Chinese eatin' wit' dat nigga?

LENNY. What?

DEMARIS. What his name, "Cheyenne"?

LENNY. Who is Cheyenne?

DEMARIS. He a nigga.

MISS REYES. He is not! He's one of those Bible people, Poppo, you know, decent, nothing to worry.

LENNY. But, Miss Reyes, that's my lady!

MISS REYES. Lissen, Poppo, I know she's your lady, but, a woman like Daisy, a little religion couldn't hurt.

DEMARIS. Look who's fuckin' talkin'.

MISS REYES. If you ask me, you deserve better, Poppo, a man with thighs like you got.

DEMARIS. You're disgusting.

MISS REYES. I'm just saying.

DEMARIS. Buy a dildo, Ma, it's cheaper.

MISS REYES. Can you believe that she came from out of my uterus, Lenny?

DEMARIS. I wanna Margarita, Ma.

MISS REYES. You thirsty, Lenny?

LENNY. Yeah.

MISS REYES. Well, we gonna take care a that! All you can drink, then, we gonna drink one more! Ay, where's the bartender, what's his name, the Irish?

LENNY. Thass what I wanna know.

MISS REYES. *(Shouts.)* Excuse me, Mr. Irish, you back there?!

DEMARIS. Less go to the other place, Ma.

MISS REYES. They don' cash my check there.

DEMARIS. So? Just blow them like you do when I'm not around.

MISS REYES. DeMaris!

DEMARIS. I'm juss playin'.

MISS REYES. Lenny doesn't know that you're just playin'!

DEMARIS. I'm juss playin', Lenny, my mother's a virgin.

MISS REYES. Where is this man? *(Shouts.)* Excuse me, please, you have customers out here waiting for ordering!

DEMARIS. I went to Spofford!

LENNY. Yeah?

DEMARIS. I fucked bitches up! Niggas try to play me, I jack them up too! I got a new hairstyle, but it's fucked up because a the rain.

MISS REYES. DeMaris, stop flirting.

DEMARIS. I ain't flirtin'!

MISS REYES. How's my son doing up there, Lenny? He's okay?

LENNY. Yeah. You should, maybe, visit him.

MISS REYES. Please. It's enough with my Husband and my grandson.

LENNY. Mr. Reyes is locked up? When's he get out?

DEMARIS. 2007.

LENNY. Thass not so bad.

MISS REYES. Please. My first man was a black, he got locked up. Then I had a Irish, they locked him up. DeMaris father was Italian, he's still locked up. Mr. Reyes can stay locked up, for all I care. You know what I'm gonna do? The next time I marry a man, it's gonna be an Indian man with his own newsstand, something nice.

DEMARIS. I wanna fuckin' drink, Ma!

MISS REYES. You juss asking for the belt tonight, aren't you?

DEMARIS. The belt? What are you, trippin'?

LENNY. Listen, why don't we go to Donnelly's, you could cash a check there.

DEMARIS. Donnelly's? That's been closed.

LENNY. They closed Donnelly's?

MISS REYES. Two years ago.

LENNY. Okay, what about we go to that old lady's joint on Fifty-fourth —

MISS REYES. — That's gone, baby.

LENNY. So, fine, we'll go to that Muggsy's, whaddya call it, Bar and Tap.

MISS REYES. Muggsy died, they making a Disney something.

LENNY. Disney?

MISS REYES. Ay, bendito, you been gone awhile.

LENNY. I thought Disney was Florida?

MISS REYES. Disney's spreading, just like the AIDS. *(Pause.)*

LENNY. Hey DeMaris, how's Wilfred, I ain't seen him.

DEMARIS. You ain't seen him 'cuz he dead.

LENNY. He's dead?

MISS REYES. Oh yeah. Mira, after he died, his mother, she got so depressed, she died. And then her husband and his brother, they went out one night, and they died — except they got killed.

LENNY. Which brother you talkin about? Carlos?

MISS REYES. Oh no, not Carlos, but he dead too.

LENNY. What?

MISS REYES. Yeah. He was doing real good, too. He finished his treatment program, and he got, like, a good job, right? So, his job, right? He was working in a lavatory for science, but he wasn't a scientist or nothing, he was a custodian, but he liked the job 'cuz you know how he was always innerested in, like, the stars and mechanics? Anyway, he was happy, and proud, too. He was walking around like his old self, you remember?

DEMARIS. Macho man.

MISS REYES. Four foot eleven in shoes, but he could carry himself, right?

DEMARIS. He was cute.

MISS REYES. Anyways, he was cleaning up the lavatory one night and he decided to mop the walk-in cooler 'cuz he was going all out on this job.

DEMARIS. Mami, tell him why they got a cooler.

MISS REYES. Because a dead brains!

LENNY. What?

MISS REYES. They do experiments on dead brains to see how they could make research. But they gotta be cold, 'cuz I don't know why.

DEMARIS. So they could be fresher.

MISS REYES. Anyway, Carlos, he opens the cooler, walks in, starts mopping, and then he dies.

LENNY. How did he die?

MISS REYES. You see, earlier, Carlos walked into the lab and saw that somebody had left out a really big piece a dry ice, like a mini iceberg. So Carlos, being Carlos, sees the dry ice getting wasted, so he drags it into the cooler and forgets about it. Later, like, hours later, he returns to mop the cooler but the dry ice, it makes gas, you know …

DEMARIS. Carbon Dioxides.

MISS REYES. The cooler was filled up with Carbon-Oxides, which is poison. And invisible! But Carlos didn't know he was walkin' into poisons 'cuz it don't smell like nothing, so he just died.

DEMARIS. Nigga died.

MISS REYES. The worst part too? He died on payday!

DEMARIS. Thass so messed up!

MISS REYES. They found the check in his pocket. He didn't even get to cash his first check.

DEMARIS. See what happens when you try to do the right thing?

LENNY. I … We, we used to play handball together. Me, Carlos, Figgy —

DEMARIS. Figgy dead too.

LENNY. What?

DEMARIS. Nah, I'm juss playin'. He at Rikers.

MISS REYES. Oh! Do you remember Mikey the Cop?

LENNY. Not dead?

DEMARIS. Nah, but he was was one of the cops who shot that black guy.

LENNY. Ya mean the black guy in the papers?

MISS REYES. No, no, not that black guy. It was … All I know, it was one of those black guys they shot (you know how they do?) like from a coupla months ago.

DEMARIS. It was longer than that.

MISS REYES. Anyways, one of the black guys who the cops shot this year, that I can't remember which one, it was Mikey who shotted him.

DEMARIS. Thass why I got a gun, so I could shoot back.

MISS REYES. Don' get me started on that gun, DeMaris! Lenny, do you think it's proper for a seventeen years old girl to carry a gun?

LENNY. I don' know.

DEMARIS. Tell him about Lucy!

LENNY. Lissen: Anything good happen while I was gone?

MISS REYES. Sure! *(Beat.)* They got a two dollah movie theatre!

15

… But now it cost three-fifty.

DEMARIS. They closing it, Ma.

MISS REYES. Don't say that!

DEMARIS. Serious. They gonna make a underground shopping mall.

MISS REYES. Thass not true!

DEMARIS. Face it bitch, it's true.

MISS REYES. DeMaris, what I told you about calling me a bitch?

DEMARIS. I'm juss saying they closing the theatre, bitch.

MISS REYES. Stop it! Juss stop it.

LENNY. DeMaris, you wanna smack? The fuck is wrong wit' you?

DEMARIS. Excuse you??!!

LENNY. Someone need to spank your ass.

DEMARIS. All I said was they closing the theatre 'cuz they closing it, and she need to deal wit' that and get a fuckin' job so we could go to the regular fuckin' theatres like regular fuckin' peoples. They closing that mothahfuckuh down, all right?!

MISS REYES. No way! I'm gonna make a complaint to Giuliani!

DEMARIS. He don' give a fuck about you.

MISS REYES. Stop with the language.

DEMARIS. They don' give a fuck about any a us niggas.

LENNY. DeMaris!

MISS REYES. Ay, where is this bartender? This is not right!

DEMARIS. Why they want a old, ugly, alcoholic bitch in their theatre for anyway? *(Miss Reyes smacks DeMaris. DeMaris punches Miss Reyes, takes out her gun.)*

DEMARIS. I'll kill you, bitch!

MISS REYES. DeMaris, stop!

DEMARIS. You don't raise your hand to me, bitch!

LENNY. DeMaris!

DEMARIS. Those days are over bitch, you got that?!

MISS REYES. I got it, I got it.

DEMARIS. Fuckin' slut. *(To Lenny.)* The fuck you lookin at?

LENNY. Thass your mother.

DEMARIS. That ain't my mother! Thass a old dried up bitch think she can still beat me down. Thass a bitch down there.

MISS REYES. Don't talk back to her, Lenny. *(DeMaris kicks Sonia.)*

16

LENNY. Hey!

DEMARIS. The fuck you gonna do? You a bitch too.

LENNY. Excuse me? *(DeMaris turns the gun on Lenny.)*

DEMARIS. You deaf, bitch? ... You gonna spank me now, Lenny? ... Lemme ax you somethin: When you was upstate, you was suckin mad dick, right?

LENNY. What?

DEMARIS. Niggas was wearin' out that ass, right? Say "Right"!

LENNY. DeMaris —

DEMARIS. Say "right." They took your ass. "Right"?

LENNY. Listen —

DEMARIS. You think I'm playin wit' you?

LENNY. No —

DEMARIS. — So answer the fuckin question. They raped you, right? Right?

LENNY. DeMaris.

DEMARIS. Say it bitch, say it!

LENNY. ... Yes.

DEMARIS. Yes, what?

LENNY. What you said ... They did.

DEMARIS. They fucked you?

LENNY. DeMaris —

DEMARIS. — For real?

LENNY. Yeah, DeMaris, for real. *(Pause.)*

DEMARIS. Swear to God?

LENNY. Yeah.

DEMARIS. They fucked a big ape like you?!

LENNY. ... I mean ... I, I fought back ... I ...

DEMARIS. Oh my Gawd!

LENNY. What?

DEMARIS. Oh my God! You so stupid!

LENNY. What?

DEMARIS. I was juss playin'.

LENNY. What?

DEMARIS. I was juss playin' and you shit your pants like a bitch!

MISS REYES. DeMaris!

DEMARIS. *(To Reyes.)* You got something to say? *(To Lenny.)* You got raped, huh?

LENNY. DeMaris …

DEMARIS. Don' worry, I ain't tellin' nobody … You a bitch, though. Get up, Ma, less go.

MISS REYES. Okay, baby.

DEMARIS. Don' forget to remind me to get the Pampers on the way home.

MISS REYES. Yes, honey … I'm sorry, Lenny. She not like this when she takes her medicat —

DEMARIS. Shut your ass! *(To Lenny.)* … You know what, though? At least the man who put his dick in your ass wasn't family. *(To Miss Reyes.)* Less go, bitch. Less go get a margarita.

MISS REYES. Yes, baby.

DEMARIS. Less go! *(They exit. Sammy is sleeping. Lenny is alone. A beat. Jake, the owner, enters from the back, sees Sammy sleeping.)*

JAKE. Hey! Hey, fuckin' Rip Van Winkle, wake up! Hey!

SAMMY. Huh?

JAKE. Get the fuck outta here!

SAMMY. Shkeckin, shiiber froo.

JAKE. This ain't a fuckin' hotel, Get out, old man!! *(To Lenny.)* This fuckin' bum, I should charge him a day rate. *(To Sammy.)* Next time you come in here, I'm gonna charge you twenty-two fifty for the day, like the fuckin' Carlton Arms! You got that, Father Time?

SAMMY. … Your father —

JAKE. — My father's dead, juss like you gonna be, any fuckin' day now.

SAMMY. This used to be a nice place.

JAKE. Yeah, then you came in. *(Sammy rises, crosses to the exit.)*

SAMMY. When you talk, I laugh.

JAKE. Well, laugh outside.

SAMMY. I'm laughin'. *(Sammy exits, Skank enters.)*

SKANK. Hey, man.

JAKE. Out!

SKANK. Right. *(Skank exits.)*

LENNY. Say, Jake, where the bartender?

JAKE. I fired his ass.

LENNY. Good.

JAKE. He's in the back, callin' Ireland, cryin'.

18

LENNY. I been tryin to get a drink for —

JAKE. Daisy Hernandez, you know her?

LENNY. Thass my girl.

JAKE. Yeah? Take her mail. Tell her she can't get her mail here no more.

LENNY. Why not?

JAKE. Making changes 'round here.

LENNY. Changes?

JAKE. Thass right. This ain't gonna be a skeeve house no more.

LENNY. Yeah?

JAKE. Dass right.

LENNY. Well, thass good. Those people, they destroy the atmosphere, right?

JAKE. *(To himself.)* Where's the friggin' key, damn it? ...

LENNY. Lemme get a, lemme get a shot a 151.

JAKE. Last call was twenty minutes ago.

LENNY. What?

JAKE. Bar is closed.

LENNY. Yeah, but —

JAKE. Bar is closed.

LENNY. Lemme juss —

JAKE. Bar is closed.

LENNY. I know, but —

JAKE. Bar is closed.

LENNY. Look —

JAKE. Bar is closed.

LENNY. You know what? You got a attitude!

JAKE. Also got a bar, and it's closed.

Scene 2

Monday morning, nine A.M. An office on 37th Street.

VIC. Siddown, Mr ...
LENNY. Lenny.
VIC. "Mr.Lenny," have a seat.
LENNY. Yes, sir ...
VIC. ... Sit ... That's some cologne you're wearing.
LENNY. Thanks, uh, you want some?
VIC. I think you got us both covered there, Lenny. Quick question: You been drinkin'?
LENNY. Uh ...
VIC. It's okay.
LENNY. Long night, but —
VIC. It's okay. If Vic says, "It's okay," then, "It's okay" ... okay?
LENNY. Um ...
VIC. Say, "Okay."
LENNY. Okay.
VIC. If we find you drinkin' on the job, you're out on your ass though, okay?
LENNY. I wouldn't do that —
VIC. So, Mr. Lenny, tell me: Why do you want to be an On-Site Field Marketeer?
LENNY. Uh, I thought this job was for handin' out flyers.
VIC. It is.
LENNY. Oh.
VIC. But it's a lot more than that, Lenny. Lemme ask you somethin, Len: Where do you see yourself in five years?
LENNY. Thass a ... I see myself ... You know what I see, uh —
VIC. Lemme tell ya a little story Len. Three years ago, I was right where you are now.
LENNY. Yeah?
VIC. Worse. Times are tough, right?

20

LENNY. A little.

VIC. Not for me, Len, not anymore, and I'll tell ya why: They took my house, they took my wife, my kids, my car, all the creature comforts, you know what they didn't take? … Ask me what they didn't take!

LENNY. What —

VIC. My initiative, Len! A man with initiative, like yourself, like me, they can't take that away. Tell me the truth: You almost didn't come right?

LENNY. It's true.

VIC. But you did come. Hey! They can send me all the college grads and M.B.A's they want, you know what I say? I say, "Send me one man with initiative, I don't want "Yale," fuck Yale! Give me one guy: School a Hard Knocks and some fire in his eye." You got that fire, Len?

LENNY. I do.

VIC. 'Cuz if you don't, please, tell me now.

LENNY. Nah, I got it.

VIC. Okay … The moustache, it goes. We like our Marketeers clean shaven.

LENNY. My moustache?

VIC. Policy … Now, hypothetical question: How many flyers you think you can hand out in ten hours?

LENNY. Uh, like a thousand?

VIC. Doesn't help me. You could hand out two thousand, three; you could toss half a them in a garbage —

LENNY. I wouldn't do that.

VIC. That's not the point. The point is: Can you get the people up here? Can you get ten people per day to come up here, apply for a credit card?

LENNY. Credit card?

VIC. You wanna hand out Chinese takeout? That's across the street. You wanna make commissions? That's here. Every person you get up here, applies for a no deposit, low interest credit card, pays the fee, and gets accepted, that's five dollars in your pocket! Get ten people, that's fifty! Get twenty people, Len, you're lookin' at hundred a day, and that's on top of your regular three bucks an hour!

LENNY. Three bucks an hour?

VIC. After training, yeah. Now, here's a piece a paper. I want you to write down the name, address, and phone number of twenty of your friends and family, anybody you know who's got bad credit.

LENNY. For what?

VIC. Every name you give me, it's like you've handed out a flyer. Anybody you know buys a credit card from us, five dollars in your pocket.

LENNY. You know what? I would prefer to just hand out the fly-ers ... With my moustache still on, if that's possible.

VIC. ... I'm sorry to hear that. Tell you what, why don't you give me a call next week?

LENNY. No, no, you don't understand. I could hand out the fly-ers, I'm good at that.

VIC. I'm sure you are. Call me next week.

LENNY. Okay, look, I'll shave the moustache, it's not a problem.

VIC. Like I said —

LENNY. I see how they hand out those flyers on the street, most a those guys, they don't do it right, I watch them —

VIC. Lenny, I got another appointment coming in.

LENNY. All right, why don't you just give me back my applica-tion fee, and I'll take off.

VIC. Non-refundable.

LENNY. What?

VIC. Is this your signature?

LENNY. Hey! Juss gimme my fuckin five dollahs back.

VIC. *(Into intercom.)* "Ray? Get Rakim and Sal in here, we got a problem with an applicant."

LENNY. Who you think you playin' wit'? Gimme my fuckin' five dollahs! *(Rakim and Sal enter.)*

RAKIM. Problem?

LENNY. What is this, a mugging?

VIC. Show Lenny the lobby.

Scene 3

Monday, late morning. The bar.

CHARLIE. Have you got a eight?

CHICKIE. No.

CHARLIE. You're supposed to say "Go Fish."

CHICKIE. Oh.

CHARLIE. Have you gotta nine?

CHICKIE. No.

CHARLIE. Chickie?!

CHICKIE. What?

CHARLIE. You gotta say, "Go Fish."

CHICKIE. Oh.

CHARLIE. So say it then.

CHICKIE. Go Fish.

CHARLIE. Your turn.

CHICKIE. Okay, um, do you have a nine?

CHARLIE. Yeah.

CHICKIE. I'll take that, thank you very much.

CHARLIE. Wait a sec, Chickie. I just axed you do you gotta nine and you said no, so how come now you gotta nine?

CHICKIE. I don't know.

CHARLIE. You do too know!

CHICKIE. No I don't.

CHARLIE. If I ax you do you got something and you got it, you gotta give it to me.

CHICKIE. Why?

CHARLIE. 'Cuz, that's the game, understand?

CHICKIE. Yeah.

CHARLIE. Okay ... You gotta Jack?

CHICKIE. No.

CHARLIE. C'mon Chickie, I know you gotta Jack.

CHICKIE. No.

CHARLIE. Chickie, look me in my eye and tell me you ain't got no Jack?

CHICKIE. … Oh, okay, here.

CHARLIE. Thank you.

CHICKIE. You happy?

CHARLIE. Yeah, I'm very happy.

CHICKIE. You don't look happy.

CHARLIE. … It's your turn.

CHICKIE. I don't wanna play. I'm hungry.

CHARLIE. You wanna eat something?

CHICKIE. Yeah.

CHARLIE. Whaddya wanna eat?

CHICKIE. Fish! Shrimps!

CHARLIE. You can't eat shrimps for breakfast. Shrimps are for lunch or dinner, not breakfast.

CHICKIE. Can I eat lunch or dinner with you?

CHARLIE. If you want.

CHICKIE. Okay.

CHARLIE. Breakfast is for Egg McMuffins and Chocolate Milk, maybe some cereals, or, like, if it's a Sunday or a special day, you could have pancakes and bacon or waffles wit' whip cream, somethin' like that. Oh! You know what?

CHICKIE. What?

CHARLIE. You could have salmon for breakfast, that's a breakfast thing.

CHICKIE. What's salmon?

CHARLIE. Whaddya mean?

CHICKIE. I mean, what's salmon?

CHARLIE. You don't know what a salmon is?

CHICKIE. What is it?

CHARLIE. A salmon is a salmon. It's a pink fish.

CHICKIE. Is it good?

CHARLIE. I don't know, but it's a fish.

CHICKIE. How about pizza?

CHARLIE. A pizza's not a fish, Chickie.

CHICKIE. Duh!! I know that! I mean, How 'bout pizza? For breakfast?

CHARLIE. Pizza for breakfast?

CHICKIE. Yeah ... Pleeeease???

CHARLIE. Okay, pizza it is.

CHICKIE. From the Arab place, okay?

CHARLIE. The Arabs?!

CHICKIE. Please??

CHARLIE. Okay, from the Arabs.

CHICKIE. Sometimes I think you're nicer than my boyfriend.

CHARLIE. I am nicer than your boyfriend.

CHICKIE. No you're not. *(Pause.)*

CHARLIE. I gotta go wash some glasses. Here's some dough for the pizza.

CHICKIE. You gotta girlfriend, Charlie?

CHARLIE. ... Yeah. I got five girlfriends.

CHICKIE. How come they never come around?

CHARLIE. 'Cuz they don' live here.

CHICKIE. Charlie? Do you think some time we could do something? I mean, not as girlfriend and boyfriend, but, like, the way we are now?

CHARLIE. Yeah, we could do that.

CHICKIE. Charlie?

CHARLIE. Yeah?

CHICKIE. How come you're so big but Jose kicked your ass, and Jimmy and Ra Ra, they kicked your ass too?

CHARLIE. I don' know.

CHICKIE. And that guy Ronnie, and that crazy guy with the hat that time, they kicked your ass too. Even my boyfriend could pro-lly kick your ass.

CHARLIE. I don't think so.

CHICKIE. Everybody always kicks his ass too, but he's little. My boyfriend, he always says, "If I was as big as that retard" —

CHARLIE. — What retard?

CHICKIE. Not you! Someone else!

CHARLIE. Who?

CHICKIE. I don' know.

CHARLIE. Lemme tell you something, Chickie ... You ever watch the *Star Wars* movies?

CHICKIE. Yeah.

CHARLIE. You know what a Jedi fighter is?

25

CHICKIE. No.

CHARLIE. Chickie, a Jedi fighter is Hans Solo and Obi Wan Kenobi and those guys over there. Even Darth Vader, you know Darth Vader?

CHICKIE. Yeah.

CHARLIE. Even he was a Jedi fighter, but he used his powers for bad, so now he gotta wear a mask and shit. Jedi fighters got powers, like, they could do anything, okay?

CHICKIE. Yeah.

CHARLIE. Ya understand?

CHICKIE. Yeah.

CHARLIE. Okay. I'm gonna tell you something, Chickie ... Me, I'm a Jedi fighter.

CHICKIE. Charlie?

CHARLIE. I'm serious, I got a Jedi name and everything. And I got powers. A lot a powers, but I can't use them for bad, or else, I gotta wear a mask like Darth Vader, and I don' think that would fly too good in the city. I got special powers, but, why am I gonna waste them on Jimmy and Jose and RaRa and those guys? I can't take the risk to lose my powers by accidently doing bad against them. But lemme tell you this: If me and you was to go out "just as friends," and somebody tried to mess wit' you or do you harm; you better believe I would use all my Jedi powers against them, even if I had to cross the line against them and do bad to them, even if I had to wear a mask for the rest a my life because a it. I wouldn't care, 'cuz you would be protected and safe, and even if they took me to jail, I would give you money first so you could go eat shrimps, okay?

CHICKIE. ... Okay.

CHARLIE. ... Okay. Go get the pizza now.

CHICKIE. Charlie?

CHARLIE. Yeah?

CHICKIE. Do you think you could show my boyfriend how to be a Jedi? Me and him, we're supposed to go to Baltimore to see his friend Jon Seda the TV and movie actor, and maybe you could come too, and you could teach him how to be a Jedi, and maybe Jon Seda, he might wanna be one too, but mostly, you could teach my boyfriend 'cuz he'd prolly be good like you if you taught him.

Could you do that?

CHARLIE. I don' know.

CHICKIE. Why not?

CHARLIE. 'Cuz my doctor over there at the place, he said that to be a Jedi fighter, you can't lie, steal, and you can't do drugs ever.

CHICKIE. Oh. *(Beat.)* I think I'll go get the pizza now.

CHARLIE. Okay.

CHICKIE. You want three Yoohoos to drink, right?

CHARLIE. Uhhuh.

CHICKIE. I'm gonna get a Diet Shasta, okay?

CHARLIE. Yeah.

CHICKIE. Can I get some gum for me and some of those little chocolate donuts for my boyfriend?

CHARLIE. Okay.

CHICKIE. Have you seen my boyfriend today?

CHARLIE. Nah.

CHICKIE. Okay.

CHARLIE. Chickie?

CHICKIE. What?

CHARLIE. … Nuttin'.

CHICKIE. Okay. *(Chickie exits. A beat.)*

SAMMY. … Shoulda shoulda.

CHARLIE. "Shoulda, shoulda," Sam?

SAMMY. What you don' tell 'em, even if they know, they still don' know … 'cept if you don' want them to know. If you don' want them to know, then they know … they always know, 'cept if they don' know, which is why you gotta tell 'em. Shoulda shoulda.

CHARLIE. Buy ya a drink, Sam?

SAMMY. Shoulda shoulda.

Scene 4

Monday night. The bar.

GREER. It was different then —

SKANK. I get ya, man. You gettin' him, there, Chickie?

CHICKIE. He's talkin' about it was different then.

GREER. I got a friend. Franklin. I call him up Friday night, and this is important, it's Friday night, okay?

SKANK. Friday night.

GREER. Not Monday, Friday! Oh! I need a drink. Barman! I'll have another, but, please, with a twist. This is not a twist, this is a wedge. Twist good, wedge bad, okay? You wanna drink?

SKANK. Sure.

GREER. Barman, one for him.

SKANK. How bout, Chickie, can she have one too?

GREER. She looks a little young.

CHICKIE. People say I look young, but then, when they see me up close, they say I don't look so young as they thought I was before they saw me up close.

GREER. Right, fine, whatever, give her a drink. So anyway, I call up my friend Franklin, "Franklin, it's been so long, blah, blah, blah, I miss you, 'I miss you too', we should get together, 'I was just thinking of you,' la la la la la." So, I say, "Where you going out tonight?" Now, lemme tell you something about Franklin. Back in the day, if you wanted a party, just look for Franklin, because, I don't care if it's the deadest night of the week, if you find Franklin, you are gonna find a party, and a damn good one too. I'm talkin about the Funhouse, Peppermint Lounge, the old Danceteria, I'm talkin bout the Limelight when the Limelight was the Limelight! Palladium, the Pyramid, I'm talkin about Studio 54. I'm talkin about doing blow with Mick Jagger and Miss Liza Minelli till eight A.M. in the back of the limo and someone's grabbin' on your you know what, and somebody's got someone's tongue in someone's

28

somethin', and everyone's feelin' it, you hear what I'm sayin?

SKANK. It's a fuckin' party.

GREER. Lord have mercy, but it was. So I says to Franklin, I says, "Whatchu doing tonight, girl?" He says, (I swear to God, if I'm lyin', I'm dyin') he says, "Well, Greer, I'm making a pot a tea and watching *The Blue Lagoon*. I says, "Creature from the Blue Lagoon"? He says, "No, Brooke Shields and Christopher Atkins *Blue Lagoon*." I says, "C'mon, girl, turn off that TV, let's do it like we used to." He start talkin 'bout AA this, "jogging" that, and do I wanna go to a "meeting." You hear what I'm sayin?

SKANK. That's rough, man.

GREER. Motherfuckah started talkin 'bout "The Lord." You feelin' me?

SKANK. Shit.

GREER. I mean, when a man start talkin' 'bout "The Lord," well, I was raised Baptist, I have heard absolutely all I need to ever hear about the damn "Lord." You wanna talk to me about "The Lord"? You better be the damn Lord — or else it's "get outta my kitchen, girl, 'cuz breakfast is definitely over!" I mean, am I wrong?

SKANK. Nah, man, I'm —

GREER. Everybody I know, it's the same shit: AA, NA, DA, GA … Name any fuckin "A," I know a motherfuckah fallin' for it. You know they got a support group for people who think they gettin' too much sex? … I mean, please. Have you ever known a man — gay, straight, whatever — have you ever had anybody, ever, come up to you talkin' about, "Oh, man, I am getting just too much booty, and the more booty I get, the more miserable I am"? Nigger, please.

SKANK. It's ridiculous.

GREER. It's depressing is what it is. Used to be, take work for example. Everybody could go out, have a good time. Now? Shit. These assholes I work with, all they wanna do is drink one Lite beer or one faggot spritzer and go home and shave their damn bodies and pump iron and eat alfalfa sprouts and meditate and watch that damn Calista Flockart skinny bitch show. You seen that show?

SKANK. Fuck that show, man.

GREER. I'll tell you right now: I never saw that show and I never will! I got better things to do with my time than watch some skinny bitch being a skinny bitch. (Pardon my language, but that's how I feel.) And I don't need "The Lord" to tell me how to feel, or what to watch, and Christopher Atkins not withstanding, I will eat a damn pussy before I stay home on Friday night makin' tea and watching the damn *Blue Lagoon*! I need a drink and I need a smoke 'cuz I'm workin' up a sweat here. What are you smokin?

SKANK. Lemme check. Chickie? What are we smokin'?

CHICKIE. We got, like, different kinds ... No, wait. We don't got different kinds. We got two Viceroys, a Merits, and a Newport, but that's for me 'cuz that's my brand. We got four cigarettes.

GREER. What's her name?

SKANK. Chickie.

GREER. Chickie, why don't you go out and pick us up a pack of Dunhills. *(To Skank.)* You like Dunhills?

SKANK. Absolutely.

GREER. They're from England, you know.

SKANK. Really?

GREER. Oh yes. All the best tobaccos, they come from England.

SKANK. Right, yeah, I heard about that.

GREER. Here's ten dollars, Chickie.

CHICKIE. They cost ten dollars?

GREER. No. Bring me the change.

CHICKIE. Okay.

SKANK. Hey Chickie, pick up a coupla a those little chocolate donuts. You know those little chocolate donuts they're like fifty-nine cents?

CHICKIE. The kind you like?

SKANK. Yeah. Those kind. *(To Greer.)* Do you mind if she picks up a coupla —

GREER. Be my guest.

CHICKIE. Can I get a Jamaican beef patty? They cost a dollar, but he gives it to me for seventy-five.

GREER. Fine, fine. But please, be quick.

CHICKIE. Okay.

SKANK. Chickie?

CHICKIE. Yeah?

SKANK. Pack a Kools.

CHICKIE. Okay.

SKANK. And a Chunky. *(To Greer.)* You like Chunky?

GREER. Sure.

SKANK. Two Chunkies. *(To Greer.)* Should you give her more money?

GREER. She has enough.

SKANK. Right.

CHICKIE. *(To Skank.)* You wanna come?

SKANK. Nah … Unless — Hey man, you feel like some blow? I know where to get some dynamite blow.

GREER. Good stuff?

SKANK. Good?! This shit is, gimme twenty dollars, I'll get us a nice bag, we'll party. You wanna party, man?

GREER. Maybe later.

SKANK. Later? See, later, they might be sold out 'cuz this stuff is like, it's really great, it's, it's, it's from fuckin', fuckin', it's from —

CHICKIE. Forty-seventh Street.

SKANK. No!! "Forty-seventh Street," listen to her. You know where it's from? It's from Peru, this shit. Peru-tian, man. Gimme thirty dollars, believe me, this coke, you do a coupla lines, you could lift a bus, man. Serious.

GREER. Why don't we let Chickie here get our cigarettes, we'll have another drink, and we'll talk about it.

SKANK. You wanna talk about it?

GREER. Is that okay with you?

SKANK. … Yeah, sure, of course.

GREER. Great, so, hurry back, Chunky.

CHICKIE. Chickie

GREER. I'm sorry, I'm thinking about that Chunky. *(To Skank.)* Excellent idea, by the way.

SKANK. What?

GREER. The Chunky.

SKANK. Oh, yeah, Chunkies, they're great. Yeah. You know what's good?

GREER. What?

CHICKIE. So, you wanna come with me?

GREER. He's staying with me.

SKANK. Yeah, baby. I'll be here.

CHICKIE. Oh … Okay. *(Chickie exits.)*

31

GREER. Barman! Another round, s'il vous plait!

SKANK. S'il vous plait, huh?

GREER. It's French. Do you speak French?

SKANK. Sometimes, yeah. *(Pause.)*

GREER. So tell me what's good.

SKANK. Huh?

GREER. You were saying …

SKANK. Oh, yeah, right. About the Chunkies. What's good is, you go to a deli, right? And you order a large hot chocolate, but you tell them to stick a Chunky in the bottom, right?

GREER. I love, love, love, love chocolate.

SKANK. Yeah. Then what you do is, you sprinkle a little blow in it and you mash up a coupla Percoset, and you stir that in too.

GREER. Oh my God! Then what?

SKANK. You drink it.

GREER. With a straw? With a spoon? What?

SKANK. I juss use my mouth.

GREER. I bet you do … Wow! … Just, "Wow!"

SKANK. Breakfast a champions —

GREER. — Can I tell you something? No, I better not. I need a smoke. I need a smoke now.

SKANK. Lemme ask Sammy. Sammy? … Sammy, got a smoke? *(To Greer.)* I'll just go through his pockets, he won't mind. *(Skank goes through Sammy's pockets, finds a pack. Sammy grabs Skank's arm and stares at him vacantly.)* Hey there, Sammy, I was just lookin for a —

SAMMY. — Whaddya wanna do, hold my hand?

SKANK. What?

SAMMY. Pat McDonagh says you'll stop asking for the money if I was to just hold your hand.

SKANK. Sammy, it's me.

SAMMY. I like whiskey, you like tea.

SKANK. Sammy, man, hey, hello?

SAMMY. I'm not Jimmy Stewart. Jimmy Stewart isn't Jimmy Stewart. You think Jimmy Stewart don't like a little ass with his biscuits?

SKANK. *(To Greer.)* Help me out, man.

GREER. Hey, mister! Can I buy you a drink?

32

SAMMY. Huh? *(Sammy releases Skank.)*
GREER. Barman, a drink for the gentlemen.
SAMMY. Thanks.
GREER. No problem.
SAMMY. … You seen my wife?
GREER. I don't know your wife.
SAMMY. I didn't ask you do you know her; I say did you see her?
SKANK. We haven't seen her.
SAMMY. Good … You sure?
SKANK. Yeah, Sam.
SAMMY. Good. Fuck her.
SKANK. Okay.
SAMMY. Don't marry a good woman.
GREER. We won't.
SAMMY. Marry a bitch, you'll sleep better. *(Pause.)*
SKANK. That old guy's got an iron grip —
GREER. — What's your name?
SKANK. My name?
GREER. Thass okay. I'm Greer.
SKANK. Hey, Greer.
GREER. I'm in real estate. You think a location like this could make money?
SKANK. Huh? Yeah, definitely.
GREER. So, What do you do?
SKANK. Me?
GREER. Actor?
SKANK. I done some acting.
GREER. I thought you looked familiar.
SKANK. Yeah. You saw *Supermen 3*?
GREER. I think so.
SKANK. I had an audition for that. What about *Gladiators*; you saw *Gladiators*, boxing movie?
GREER. You know what? Yes. I saw that.
SKANK. Okay, in the beginning, when the Spanish kid with the rat tail, when he starts fighting and he beats that white guy with the tattoo?
GREER. Yeah?
SKANK. That's me, man.

GREER. Really?

SKANK. Look, see, here's my tattoo. In real life, the scene, it was longer, but in the movie it was like, "There I am, boom! I'm down!" You know that show *Homicide*? The kid with the rat tail, he's on that show. He's a friend of mine. Jon Seda, man.

GREER. I don't know him, but, I bet you're a lot better than him.

SKANK. Yeah, well, nah, he's a good guy. I'm supposed to go see him, me and Chickie, we're supposed to go for, like, a visit, but, like, you know, schedules and shit. You think you could gimme twenty dollars?

GREER. For what?

SKANK. I'll come right back,

GREER. You'll come back?

SKANK. I juss gotta pick up this prescription, over at the Rite Aid —

GREER. — Prescription?

SKANK. Yeah, it's my aunt. She gotta disease, man, it's bad.

GREER. What kinda disease?

SKANK. It's really bad, man. It's … a bad one.

GREER. Look, it's not that I don't trust you —

SKANK. — Greer, man, I'll pay ya back. My friend, he's comin' by, he's supposed to be here, he got money, he owes me money, he's rich! Maybe you know him. Nic Cage, the actor?

GREER. Nic Cage is comin' here?

SKANK. Yeah, man. We took a class together.

GREER. You're fuckin' cute, you know that?

SKANK. Yeah?

GREER. With your bitchin' little body. Lemme see your abs.

SKANK. Hey, man.

GREER. You want twenty dollars? Lemme see your abs. *(Skank lifts his shirt.)*

GREER. Nice.

SKANK. You like that?

GREER. Yeah.

SKANK. I look good, right?

GREER. Okay, I give you twenty dollars, whatchu gonna give me?

SKANK. Hey, man, I'm not takin' the money, I'm juss borrowing

34

it. My friend's —

GREER. — Yeah, yeah, "Nic Cage, sick aunt, suck my dick kiss my ass," okay? I give you twenty dollahs, whatchu gonna give me?

SKANK. Lissen, man —

GREER. — Okay, goodnight. *(Greer goes to leave.)*

SKANK. Wait, wait, wait! Siddown!

GREER. Talk to me, girl.

SKANK. ... Shit, man! What happened to trust, dude? What happened to taking a man at his word?

GREER. I sat back down for this?

SKANK. I'm juss sayin —

GREER. — You think you the only piece a ass on this street? I'll walk out that door right now and I'll find younger, better looking, and better abs.

SKANK. So go then.

GREER. No. I'm gonna hear you out, 'cuz you got nice eyes. You got nice eyes, you know that?

SKANK. You like my eyes?

GREER. Your eyes got tragedy in them.

SKANK. Tragedy?

GREER. Tragedy's sexy ... Talk to me, tragedy, do business with me.

SKANK. Okay ... first of all, forget twenty dollahs, okay?

GREER. It's forgotten.

SKANK. Sixty dollahs.

GREER. Sixty dollahs for what?

SKANK. Okay. Sixty dollahs, we go to the bathroom.

GREER. Okay.

SKANK. I do a little show.

GREER. What kinda show?

SKANK. A sexy show.

GREER. Yeah?

SKANK. I'll gyrate, I'll touch myself.

GREER. Speak English.

SKANK. Okay, I'll jerk off for you. You can jerk off too.

GREER. Sixty dollars so I could jerk myself off? I could do that at home for free watchin the damn *Blue Lagoon.*

SKANK. Yeah, but with me, you get me.

GREER. Can I touch you?

SKANK. No.

GREER. You must be joking.

SKANK. Okay, you can touch me a little. My chest, my arms.

GREER. Your ass?

SKANK. Sorry, man. You can't touch my ass.

GREER. Forget it then.

SKANK. You wanna touch my ass? For eighty, you can touch it.

GREER. Eighty dollars to touch your ass?

SKANK. I'm givin' you a competitive price.

GREER. For eighty dollars I'm entering that ass! For eighty dollahs, that ass gonna hail me a cab home, tip the driver, and cook me breakfast in bed the next morning.

SKANK. I don't think you're aware of the current marketplace —

GREER. — Lemme tell you something about the marketplace, girl —

SKANK. — I'm not a girl —

GREER. — I'm sorry, baby —

SKANK. — I'm not a baby and I am not a fuckin' girl! You wanna talk business, let's talk business! Eighty dollars.

GREER. You wanna talk business?

SKANK. Thass what I'm sayin'.

GREER. I'm gonna put it like this: Twenty dollars, we go into the bathroom, you suck my dick.

SKANK. Suck your dick? Dude, you're outta your mind.

GREER. Is this a racial thing?

SKANK. Fuck you, man.

GREER. Goodnight!

SKANK. Look, uh, if you want a blow job, Chickie'll do that for you.

GREER. Chickie? What the hell I want with Chickie?

SKANK. You wanna blow job, Chickie blows.

GREER. Chickie ain't comin' back.

SKANK. Yeah she is.

GREER. How many crackheads you know, you give 'em a ten dollar bill, they gonna come back?

SKANK. Look man, if I say Chickie's comin back, then, she's comin' back.

GREER. We goin' to the bathroom or not?

SKANK. Look —

GREER. — Goodnight!

SKANK. Wait!

GREER. I said, goodnight sweet prince, this show is over!

SKANK. Fuck!!!

GREER. … What?

SKANK. Fuck!! … *(Pause.)* … Okay, I'll do it.

GREER. You gonna do it?

SKANK. Forty bucks, I'll jerk you off.

GREER. Twenty bucks.

SKANK. Thirty-five bucks, I'll jerk you, you can touch my ass.

GREER. Twenty bucks.

SKANK. Fuck, man. Thirty bucks, okay? Thirty. That's it. Thirty.

GREER. Twenty bucks.

SKANK. This is bullshit, man. You know who I am? You know where I been? I was in the army, man. I was in *Hamlet*! Fuckin' *Hamlet*! I did a commercial, man. I saved a kid once. I took a kid outta a burnin' crack house, risked my life! If I had money and someone needed it, I'd give it to him! I give money to people all the time! I let Chickie sell my last bag last week, my last bag. Do you know what that is to give someone your last fuckin' bag??!! How many of these scumbags out here would do that, huh? You know why I did it man? 'Cuz I got the human compassion, man! I got the love in me, I got love! Love! What you got, man? What the hell you got?

GREER. You know what I got? I got twenty bucks … Whatchu gonna do? *(Pause.)*

SKANK. Let's go, man. Let's do it.

GREER. What're we gonna do?

SKANK. What you want.

GREER. Look me in my eyes … You know what I want to do?

SKANK. Just do it, okay? I don' wanna hear it, I just wanna do it. Give the bartender five bucks, he'll keep the bathroom clear.

GREER. Fine.

SKANK. You get fifteen minutes, man.

GREER. Don' worry, baby. What I wanna do ain't gonna take but five.

ACT TWO

Scene 1

Eighth Avenue. Tuesday, late morning.

CHICKIE. You gotta smile.

DEMARIS. For what?

CHICKIE. Watch. Do like I do, okay? *(To a Man.)* "Hey, baby!" *(To DeMaris.)* You gotta be like that. Like you're a party waitin' to happen. *(To another Man.)* "Hey, baby!" *(To DeMaris.)* Think about money.

DEMARIS. I'm a bank some "Benji's" tonight!

CHICKIE. Yeah, that's better. You doin' better.

DEMARIS. Yeah?

CHICKIE. But smile, like you know a secret.

DEMARIS. Yeah. Yeah. I'm wid dat!

CHICKIE. That's good! *(To Man #1)* "Hey, Baby."

MAN #1. *(To DeMaris.)* I like that ass.

DEMARIS. Fuck you, bitch!!! *(Man #1 hurries off.)* You bettah run, little punk ass bitch!! *(To Chickie.)* Oh, shit! You see dat nigga run?

CHICKIE. DeMaris!

DEMARIS. I'm sorry.

CHICKIE. They're not supposed to be running away from us, DeMaris.

DEMARIS. How you gonna let a man disrespect us like that?!

CHICKIE. You know what? I think this is a bad idea.

DEMARIS. I said I was sorry, Chickie.

CHICKIE. No. It's good that you're like that. It's just not good if you wanna make money.

DEMARIS. I wanna make money. I wanna make money for me

38

and my baby.

CHICKIE. You mean your boyfriend?

DEMARIS. My boyfriend? Fuck that nigga! I'm talkin 'bout my baby, my blood.

CHICKIE. You mean like a kid?

DEMARIS. You nevah seent my baby? Look, thass my baby, thass Evan. Thass a nice name, right?

CHICKIE. Oh! ... He's ... he's cute.

DEMARIS. Right?

MAN #2. Hey there, ladies —

DEMARIS. Get the fuck out my face, you wanna get shot? *(Man #2 hurries off.)*

CHICKIE. DeMaris!

DEMARIS. He was tryin' to get all up in my face.

CHICKIE. Yeah? So?

DEMARIS. Dat don't sit wit' me.

CHICKIE. I'm sorry DeMaris, but, I don't get from you that you have what it takes to trick.

DEMARIS. So teach me.

CHICKIE. I did teach you.

DEMARIS. So teach me again.

CHICKIE. DeMaris, it's not the worst thing in the world to be not good at this. It's prolly a good thing.

DEMARIS. No it ain't.

CHICKIE. There's alot a others things you could prolly do. Like ... rob!

DEMARIS. Nah, 'cuz, they say if I get locked up again, they gonna take Evan from me.

CHICKIE. But you could get locked up doin' this.

DEMARIS. But I heard the cops is friendly.

CHICKIE. Sometimes.

DEMARIS. I need ta make some bank, Chickie. I need ta make a place that ain't my mothah's place. I need ta be a mothah to my kid. I need bank.

CHICKIE. DeMaris —

DEMARIS. I'll do whatevah you say, and I won't curse out no more peoples. I ain't tryin' to come to you wrong, I'm juss axin' you as a friend.

CHICKIE. As a friend?

DEMARIS. What are you sayin', that you ain't my friend?

CHICKIE. DeMaris, you pulled a gun on me, that's the only reason I'm doin' this.

DEMARIS. So then, what? You don't like me?

CHICKIE. You pulled a gun on me!

DEMARIS. I was juss playin', Chickie, I wouldn't have shotted you or nuthin'.

CHICKIE. That's not what you said before.

DEMARIS. Okay, so I apologize okay?

CHICKIE. DeMaris —

DEMARIS. Here. Take my gun … nah for real, take it. I got my initials on there, see?

CHICKIE. Yeah.

DEMARIS. Thass cool, right? You could keep it, like, as a gift. You to me … You like my coat?

CHICKIE. Yeah.

DEMARIS. Try it on.

CHICKIE. DeMaris —

DEMARIS. Juss try it on. It's nice, right?

CHICKIE. Yeah.

DEMARIS. Dass 'cuz it's name brand!

CHICKIE. It's furry inside.

DEMARIS. You could have it, okay?

CHICKIE. You mean, like "have it" have it?

DEMARIS. … Lissen, mama … I'm sorry about, like, threatenin' your life and shit. Okay?

CHICKIE. Okay.

DEMARIS. Dat ain't me. I mean, it is me, but … you know the dilly, right?

CHICKIE. It's okay, DeMaris.

DEMARIS. So you could teach me now?

CHICKIE. I just really need to get high, you know?

DEMARIS. You could take my chain and pawn it. Here, take it.

CHICKIE. Do I have ta pay you back?

DEMARIS. Are you my friend?

CHICKIE. Yeah —

DEMARIS. — Then you don' haveta! We friends now, okay?

CHICKIE. Okay

DEMARIS. We niggas, right?

CHICKIE. Yeah.

DEMARIS. And if a nigga's my friend, Chickie, then I got that nigga's back. I want you to know that. And even though you ain't really down, I still consider you as down, 'cuz you good people, you a friend. And if a nigga's a friend, then I put them in the books for life. I put them ahead a everybody, even family, 'cuz they the real family, know what I'm sayin', Chickie? *(Pause.)*

CHICKIE. Do you know who Jon Seda is?

DEMARIS. You mean that fine nigga from TV?

CHICKIE. My boyfriend knows him.

DEMARIS. Yeah?

CHICKIE. I spoke to him on the phone one time, he sounds just like on TV.

DEMARIS. He fine.

CHICKIE. Me and my boyfriend, we're gone leave here soon and go be with Jon Seda.

DEMARIS. For real?

CHICKIE. Yup.

DEMARIS. I could come too?

CHICKIE. I gotta ask my boyfriend first, that is if I can find him, but, yeah, maybe.

DEMARIS. I could bring Evan?

CHICKIE. Yeah.

DEMARIS. Jon Seda got like a mansion, right?

CHICKIE. He's got a built in pool!

DEMARIS. For real? We could swim in there?

CHICKIE. Thing is, we gotta save money, 'cuz, you know how guys are, they don't save good.

DEMARIS. How much you got saved?

CHICKIE. Right now? Nothin'. I mean, I had something saved before, but, I had to make an emergency purchase 'cuz, well, I ended up smoking it, but, like, if me and you teamed up, we could be on the road with my boyfriend and Evan prolly like in a month.

DEMARIS. I like the way that sounds, "On the Road." You mean like in a car, right?

CHICKIE. Yeah.

DEMARIS. Mercedes?

CHICKIE. Or a Ford.

DEMARIS. "Built ta last," right? And we could drink champagne in the car and play games?

CHICKIE. Yeah. And we could stay in motels.

DEMARIS. Thass like a hotel, right?

CHICKIE. Do you like poems?

DEMARIS. Yeah.

CHICKIE. We could make up some poems in the car, like, poems about things.

DEMARIS. And eat chocolate!

CHICKIE. I'm thinkin' that when we get to Jon Seda's —

DEMARIS. I'm gonna fuck that nigga, watch!

CHICKIE. We could be like two couples.

DEMARIS. You seen Jon Seda's ass in *Primal Fear*? Dat shit is clean.

CHICKIE. You ever smoke crack?

DEMARIS. Nah ... but don't tell nobody.

CHICKIE. See, the truth is, DeMaris ... you're really bad at this, but, if you smoke a little crack, it's gonna take the edge off your ... edge ... ya know?

DEMARIS. Okay.

CHICKIE. Especially when you're just startin' out, like you. It helps.

DEMARIS. So less go get some.

CHICKIE. ... I'm a crackhead, you know that, right? I'm a pretty good crackhead, but still ...

DEMARIS. So? I still like you.

CHICKIE. But if you smoke crack, ya know, people get addicted.

DEMARIS. I won't.

CHICKIE. No, but you might ...

DEMARIS. I swear ta God I won't get addicted.

CHICKIE. Well ...

DEMARIS. C'mon, Chickie, please????

CHICKIE. Well, here's the only thing I'm thinkin, when we get to Jon Seda's, he's rich so he could send us to Betty Ford, and we could get clean and quit for real and then we'd be just healthy and tan all the time and hang out with my boyfriend and Jon Seda.

DEMARIS. Don Johnson goes to Betty Ford, right?

CHICKIE. I think so.

DEMARIS. Ah-aight, I'll go. Not to fuck him or nuttin', but juss to, like, hang out, smoke a blunt. Take a photo.

CHICKIE. Okay.

DEMARIS. Lissen: Gimme back the chain. I'll pawn it and pick up some rock, okay?

CHICKIE. I could go.

DEMARIS. Nah, but, my friend, he could sell it to me cheaper, we could get bettah value like that.

CHICKIE. Okay.

DEMARIS. I'll be right back.

CHICKIE. Okay.

DEMARIS. Wait for me.

CHICKIE. Okay.

DEMARIS. You're gonna wait for me?

CHICKIE. Yup.

DEMARIS. I'll be right back.

CHICKIE. Okay.

DEMARIS. You gonna wait for me, right?

CHICKIE. Uh-huh.

DEMARIS. You my nigga, Chickie.

CHICKIE. You too.

DEMARIS. I'll be back like in ten minutes, maybe.

CHICKIE. Okay.

DEMARIS. You gonna be here when I get back, right?

CHICKIE. Yup.

DEMARIS. For real?

CHICKIE. Yes, DeMaris, for real.

DEMARIS. Ah-aight.

CHICKIE. Okay.

DEMARIS. Bye.

CHICKIE. Bye.

DEMARIS. I'll be right back.

CHICKIE. Okay.

DEMARIS. Wait for me. *(DeMaris exits. Chickie lights a cigarette, smokes. Holy Roller enters.)*

CHICKIE. Hi baby.

HOLY ROLLER. Are you lost?

CHICKIE. Yeah.

HOLY ROLLER. God loves the lost.

CHICKIE. Yeah?

HOLY ROLLER. Yes ma'am, he does.

CHICKIE. What about you, mister? You love the lost?

HOLY ROLLER. Me?

CHICKIE. You a cop?

HOLY ROLLER. No.

CHICKIE. You wanna go somewhere and save me?

HOLY ROLLER. I ...

CHICKIE. Uh-huh.

HOLY ROLLER. ... I got a room, coupla blocks.

CHICKIE. Hundred dollars. Okay?

HOLY ROLLER. Okay.

CHICKIE. Money now, mister.

HOLY ROLLER. *(Opens his wallet.)* Three hundred dollars. Does that buy the afternoon?

CHICKIE. *(Takes the money.)* Let's go.

HOLY ROLLER. ... Jesus himself laid down with whores and sinners; serpents and snakes, people like you.

CHICKIE. I like Jesus.

HOLY ROLLER. ... "And the last shall be first." What's your name?

CHICKIE. Barbara.

HOLY ROLLER. You shall be first, Barbara.

CHICKIE. Okay.

Scene 2

The bar, Tuesday afternoon.

DAISY. They threw out the jukebox?

JAKE. Hey, they got CD jukeboxes now.

DAISY. But it sound better when you could hear the record scratching.

JAKE. You people ruined that jukebox.

DAISY. Don't put me in wit' those other people.

JAKE. This fuckin' stain! Goddamn Chinks, I'm gonna shove this suit up their ass! Twelve dollahs for dry cleaning, and look at this! I look like I pissed myself.

DAISY. Lemme take a look, baby. *(Daisy bends down to examine the crotch stain.)*

JAKE. Twelve dollahs! The fuck does he get off thinkin' he can charge twelve bucks? ... Yuppie Chink fuck! *(To Daisy.)* Hey, hey! Ease off! Not in front of The Walking Dead over there. *(To Sam.)* Hey! Whistler's Mother! When you finish suckin' on that ice, it's goodbye time.

SAMMY. ... The hobos, if ya gave them food, they'd put an "X" wit' chalk on your stoop so's another hobo would know it. They'd put an "X" —

JAKE. — Yeah yeah, "X" this. *(To Daisy.)* Jesus Christ, look at this, this is supposed to be my Florida suit.

DAISY. You ain't goin' to Florida.

JAKE. Watch me!

DAISY. With your wife, right?

JAKE. Daisy, how many times we gotta plough the same field? Yes, wit' my wife. I got a wife, at least for now. I leave my wife now, whaddya think happens? She takes everything, I end up on a park bench wit' you and your pals. Not me sister, I got bigger fish to fry.

DAISY. What about me?

JAKE. What about you?

45

DAISY. How you gonna act like that to me?

JAKE. Lissen, toots, I'm in a state a aggravation here, okay?

DAISY. You ain't sensitive to my feelings, Jake.

JAKE. Okay, you know what? If I wanted someone wit' feelings, I'd get one who I could take out in public! How's that?! ... Ya see what ya made me do? Ya see how ya made me stoop? I need a broad's gonna bring me back up to my level, not drag me down to hers.

DAISY. It's like dat, huh?

JAKE. Sweetheart, look, why can't we enjoy the time we got now?

DAISY. I'm tired a you threatenin' Florida on me.

JAKE. I'm sorry, okay? Lissen to me now: I made a reservation at the place you like, the Sizzler, and I'll tell ya what: I'll reserve the room till noon tomorrow, okay? We'll stay up late, make fun of the pornos like we usedta, make a night a it ... Whaddya say, Peaches? ... Say, you like the dress I got you?

DAISY. Do you like it?

JAKE. Like it? I can't wait to rip it off you! Lemme go back, get the keys, make a call, be back in a sec.

DAISY. Whatever.

JAKE. Have a drink if ya like. *(Jake exits to back. A beat. Daisy pours a drink. Lenny enters.)*

LENNY. Hey honey, I seen you through the window.

DAISY. Whaddya mean?

LENNY. Sittin' here wit' Sammy. *(To Sammy.)* Sam-my! Que Pasa? *(To Daisy.)* Hey, thass a beautiful dress.

DAISY. Lenny —

LENNY. Don't say it! Hey, the mirror is gone.

DAISY. Yeah.

LENNY. I miss you; I would like ta tell dat to you.

DAISY. Look —

LENNY. Lissen, I gotta coupla dollahs from my moms, why don' we get a coupla slices, go to that cheap movie theatre I been hearin' about?

DAISY. Lenny —

LENNY. Lissen, this ain't easy for me to say, but — *(Jake enters from the back.)*

JAKE. Okay, Peaches. Let's roll.

46

LENNY. Peaches?? *(To Daisy.)* What's, what's goin' on?

DAISY. Nuthin'.

LENNY. How come you two's dressed like that?

DAISY. Lenny, it's not what you think.

LENNY. Think? Think what?

JAKE. *(To Lenny.)* Hey, bozo, take a hike!

LENNY. Who you callin bozo??!!

JAKE. Say it walkin' buddy.

LENNY. Why don't you make me? *(To Daisy.)* Wha, what is this?

DAISY. You've been gone six years, Lenny.

LENNY. So?

DAISY. So I gotta have a life too.

LENNY. Yeah, but ... Him??!! Him??!!

DAISY. I love him.

LENNY. You love me.

DAISY. I need a man, Lenny.

JAKE. Last warning, pal.

LENNY. *(To Jake.)* You shut up! Just, shut up! *(To Daisy.)* You sayin' I ain't a fuckin' man? Dat what you think a me?

DAISY. I need a man, Lenny.

JAKE. All right that's it.

LENNY. *(To Jake.)* Wait a second! *(To Daisy.)* You want a man? I'll show you a man! I'm gonna get a job, and some money, and we gonna, we gonna go out! I'm a take you for a steak dinner and, and, then we gonna see a show; and I'm a take you on a horse and buggy through Central Park wit' a blanket ta keep us warm! Then, when we back together, I'm a come back and put a bullet in this motherfuckah's head right here! Count on it!

JAKE. You wanna do it now?

LENNY. Count on it!

JAKE. You ain't doin' shit.

DAISY. Jake!

JAKE. Big talk, zero action! You ain't gonna do a damn thing. Why? 'Cuz you ain't shit! I seen thousands like you, thirty years in this sewer! You know what you are? You're garbage, pal. Loser garbage. Look at me! You should jump in the friggin' Hudson, sink to the bottom wit' the rest of the crap, ya pussy. Do decent people a favor. Get outta here! Go! ... (Jesus Christ, look at my

47

suit, I swear ta God I'm goin to Florida)!

DAISY. Jake —

JAKE. You people got some surprises in store. Peaches, get me a little more club soda, eh?

DAISY. Jake, you hurt him.

JAKE. And what? You didn't? Fuck this noise. *(Jake exits.)*

DAISY. Jake! *(To Lenny.)* You mess up everything. *(Daisy runs out calling for Jake. A beat.)*

SAMMY. ... They put an "X" wit' the chalk, juss like that, Gladdis ... "X."

Scene 3

Tuesday night. Eighth Avenue. Demaris, alone and wasted.

DEMARIS. Who wanna buy some pussy up in this mother-fuckah?! Who wanna work my middle tonight? ... Y'all a bunch a punk ass bitches!! *(A man walks by.)* 'Scuse me sir. Sir! You wanna blaze my ass? ... How bout I suck your little tiny pinga *(Man hurries off.)* Faggot! Little Punk! ... Shit ... *(A woman walks by.)* 'Scuse me bitch, you a lesbian? You want a little choacha? *(Woman hurries off.)* S'matter, bitch? You know you want it! *(A man walks by.)* The fuck you lookin at, nigga? You nevah saw no ho before? Go home ta your mama, bitch! *(Demaris starts singing a song like Boyz2Men's "Mama."* A beat. A man approaches.)*

CARROLL. You got a nice voice.

DEMARIS. Shut up, I'm singin'. *(DeMaris sings a bit more, then stops abruptly.)* Dat was [Boyz2Men].

CARROLL. That was great.

DEMARIS. Hi.

CARROLL. Hi.

DEMARIS. Um, hi.

CARROLL. Whaddya doin?

* See Special Note on Songs and Recordings on copyright page.

48

DEMARIS. Um, nothin', but, um, I'm smilin', I wish Chickie could see, I'm smilin', right?

CARROLL. Yes you are.

DEMARIS. I got criticized earlier, before, for not smilin', but now, I'm smilin', right?

CARROLL Hey, you got me smilin' now.

DEMARIS. I got a good smile, right? Does it look like I know a secret or some shit?

CARROLL. It looks pretty.

DEMARIS. Thank you, thass a nice compliment, uh ...

CARROLL. So, whaddya up to?

DEMARIS. Um, yeah, like, you cute and shit.

CARROLL. Thank you.

DEMARIS. So, like, "you wanna party?"

CARROLL. What kinda party?

DEMARIS. You know, like, fucking?

CARROLL. Hey, you cut right to the chase, don't you?

DEMARIS. Yeah, I'm like that. So, you wanna fuck me?

CARROLL. For free?

DEMARIS. No stupid, not for free. Sorry, I didn't mean "stupid" like that, I juss meant not the "for free" part. You know what I'm sayin'? 'Cuz like, I tell you right now, I could fuck like a mothah-fucker, wear a nigga out, know I'm sayin'? You cute, though. I like the way you, yeah ...

CARROLL. So, how much?

DEMARIS. How much you wanna spend?

CARROLL. I'm flexible.

DEMARIS. You bettah be flexible, 'cuz, I'll wear your ass out wit' like positions and shit —

CARROLL. Name your price.

DEMARIS. Ah-aight ... How bout a "G"? Thousand dollars, you could have this ass, plus ... plus ... look! I got some crack. You smoke crack? And also I got a blunt somewhere, where it go? Here it is!! It's good too, chronic! One "G," I'll get ya high and fuck ya dry ... thass a rhyme! Look at my ass! Thass a ass right there! Thousand dollahs, you can have it! Whaddya say? You got a light?

CARROLL. Sorry sweetie.

DEMARIS. The fuck you doin'? Get ya hands off me, nigga!

49

CARROLL. Hit me, it gets ugly quick.

DEMARIS. Fuck you, bitch! Ow, nigga! That hurts!

CARROLL. Let's go.

DEMARIS. Lemme get my cigarette.

CARROLL. I'll get you another in the precinct, how's that?

DEMARIS. Precinct?!

CARROLL. What are you doin' out on a school night anyway?

DEMARIS. Please don't take me to no precinct, mistah.

CARROLL. Better I should leave you out here so you could end up like that girl we found in the dumpster?

DEMARIS. But they gonna take my baby if you bust me.

CARROLL. Maybe they should.

DEMARIS. Dat ain't right what you said, Mister! Dat ain't right!

CARROLL. C'mon kid, this is like going to the doctor; we give ya a lollipop when it's all over.

DEMARIS. Hold up a minute!

CARROLL. Pop Tarts and Apple Jacks at the station house, let's go.

ACT THREE

Scene 1

The bar. Wednesday morning.

DAISY. Hey, Charlie, how you doin'?

CHARLIE. Good.

DAISY. I could get a Bacardi?

CHARLIE. Nah.

DAISY. Charlie, I wasn't axing it like a question. Gimme a Bacardi.

CHARLIE. I can't.

DAISY. Why not?

CHARLIE. It ain't twelve.

DAISY. C'mon.

CHARLIE. You know I can't serve before twelve.

DAISY. What about Sammy there, he got a drink.

CHARLIE. Yeah, but he's old.

DAISY. So?

CHARLIE. So, he's old. He could drop any minute, like this, he won't go thirsty.

DAISY. Gimme a Bacardi in a coffee cup then.

CHARLIE. You make my job hard, Daisy.

DAISY. Yeah, well, it's a hard world. *(Charlie pours her a drink.)*

CHARLIE. Three dollars.

DAISY. You could put it on a tab?

CHARLIE. No more tabs, Jake said.

DAISY. Why not?

CHARLIE. 'Cuz he said it.

DAISY. But why?

CHARLIE. I ain't tellin'.

51

DAISY. Tellin' what?

CHARLIE. The thing I ain't tellin'.

DAISY. Lemme get another.

CHARLIE. You ain't paid for the first one.

DAISY. I bet if Chickie wanted one, you'd give her the whole bottle.

CHARLIE. No.

DAISY. 'Cuz you like her.

CHARLIE. No.

DAISY. I'm gonna tell her!

CHARLIE. C'mon, Daisy.

DAISY. Lemme get a double then. *(Charlie pours a double.)*

CHARLIE. I like you a lot better when you ain't like this.

DAISY. You seen Lenny?

CHARLIE. Nah.

DAISY. He didn't come home lass night.

CHARLIE. Maybe he got caught up.

DAISY. I guess. How 'bout Jake? You seen him?

CHARLIE. Not yet … nine dollars.

DAISY. Charlie.

CHARLIE. C'mon Daisy: three drinks, nine dollars.

DAISY. So, if I had three drinks, then where my free one at?

CHARLIE. You gotta pay for three to get one free.

DAISY. So lemme pay you in the back.

CHARLIE. Nah.

DAISY. You don' wanna touch my titties?

CHARLIE. C'mon, Daisy.

DAISY. Wha? You don' like my titties no more?

CHARLIE. Nah, Daisy. It ain't nuttin' against your titties.

DAISY. So, what is it?

CHARLIE. It's things. Things is changin'.

DAISY. What things?

CHARLIE. Besides that, it ain't right. It ain't right for, you know, it ain't right.

DAISY. You sayin' you better than me?

CHARLIE. Nah, Daisy. I ain't better than you and those people out there, they ain't better than us. Probably, I'll miss your titties. I like 'em.

DAISY. Why you gonna miss 'em, they ain't goin nowhere?

CHARLIE. Forget it, Daisy. I'll juss put the money in the register myself.

DAISY. You don't gotta pay for me! I pay my own way!

CHARLIE. So, then ... ah, forget it.

DAISY. Here.

CHARLIE. What's this?

DAISY. It's a toaster.

CHARLIE. Where'd you get it?

DAISY. My friend gave it to me.

CHARLIE. What's it do?

DAISY. It makes toast, the fuck you think it does?

CHARLIE. I get my toast from the deli, Daisy.

DAISY. What's goin on 'round here, Charlie?

CHARLIE. Nuttin'.

DAISY. You ain't my friend no more!

CHARLIE. I am too, Daisy.

DAISY. No you ain't.

CHARLIE. I am too!

DAISY. Fuckin' Lenny, Fuckin' Jake, Fuckin' you. Thass okay, though. I know who my friends is. *(Pause.)*

SAMMY. Gladdis!!

CHARLIE. Yeah, Sammy?

SAMMY. More tea!

CHARLIE. You want beer tea or whiskey tea, Sammy? ... Sammy?

SAMMY. I'm talkin' about the day they moved the Dodgers outta Brooklyn ...

CHARLIE. Talkin' to who?

SAMMY. Spit shine. I got my first spit shine with the old man, spit shine, shot a whiskey, Roy Campanella ... Campy ...

CHARLIE. Thass good, Sam

SAMMY. Mickey Owen come on my bus, I wouldn't let him on.

CHARLIE. Yeah?

SAMMY. I says, "You think about what you done, Mick, you think about it."

DAISY. Charlie, please, stop talkin' to that fool.

SAMMY. *(To Daisy.)* Huh?

53

DAISY. Ah, fuck ... Hi, Sam.

SAMMY. Marisol?

DAISY. Marisol?

SAMMY. *(To Charlie.)* My wife here?

CHARLIE. Nah, Sammy.

SAMMY. If my wife was to come in here now, oh boy! ... Oh, boy!

CHARLIE. I got ya covered Sammy.

SAMMY. Ya do?

CHARLIE. I got lookouts on both sides a Forty-third Street.

SAMMY. You look beautiful, Marisol.

DAISY. Thank you.

SAMMY. You look even more beautiful than I remember. How'd ya get so beautiful?

DAISY. I don't know, Sam.

SAMMY. "It's better to light one up than to curse the darkness." Remember that, Marisol?

DAISY. Okay.

SAMMY. You gotta nice shape, Marisol.

DAISY. Thank you.

SAMMY. Don't tell my wife.

CHARLIE. We won't, Sam.

SAMMY. You seen my wife?

CHARLIE. I think she's at the A&P. *(Pause.)*

SAMMY. She's not at the A&P, Charlie. *(To Daisy.)* I'm gonna light a candle for ya, Marisol.

DAISY. Okay.

SAMMY. I gotta light a candle for Gladdis first, but then I'm gonna light one for you 'cuz you're more beautiful than I remembered.

DAISY. Thanks, Sam.

SAMMY. And what I remembered was pretty good. Beautiful ... beautiful ... I wish we lived in Arabia ...

DAISY. What?

SAMMY. Arabia ... *(He drifts off.)*

DAISY. Charlie?

CHARLIE. Here, Daisy. One on me. *(Greer enters with a fashionable looking gentlemen.)*

GREER. *(Talking to his friend.)* See the bar? It's genuine antique oak from 1937, feel how sturdy, smooth? But fuck it, I want it outta here. The fixtures are for shit, but look at the moldings. Nice, right? They can stay, maybe. This wall's coming down, and that! what do you call that thing? Anyway, garbage! Oh, and they got a great bathroom in the back … Okay, the walls: lime! I want everything lime! You wanna drink? *(To Charlie.)* Barman! Two Herrendura frozen margaritas, light salt, heavy lime, make it with Cointreau. *(To his friend.)* That's French, you know.

CHARLIE. Uh, we don' make that, we ain't got it.

GREER. *(To his friend.)* See what I mean? *(To Charlie.)* Fine, fine. Two beers. Cold. You got cold beer?

CHARLIE. Yeah.

GREER. Good. And take down that soccer poster, whatever it is, it's hurting my eyes.

SAMMY. In Arabia, you can have two wives. *(To Charlie.)* One for you and one for me. *(To Daisy.)* And one for you, Marisol. Beautiful.

GREER. *(To his friends.)* I'm thinkin' about keepin the ol' man. Put him in a tux, you know, for atmosphere?

SAMMY. In Arabia … we'd all be kings!

Scene 2

Wednesday night. A park bench near the West Side Highway. Skank is nodding. Charlie enters holding a bag with a Darth Vader mask in it.

CHARLIE. Wake up, fuckin' junkie. Wake up, Skell.

SKANK. Huh?

CHARLIE. You shoulda been there for her. You shoulda protected her.

SKANK. Huh?

CHARLIE. They got her on a fuckin' table all cut up and naked,

55

I was there. Where the fuck were you? You were being a fuckin'
lowlife piece a shit junkie, thass where you was.

SKANK. Wha?

CHARLIE. You ain't gonna live another day, thass for sure. Thass
the least I could do, you fuckin' bastid! *(Charlie attacks Skank.)*
You think it's funny? You think this is a friggin' joke? I brung her
shrimps! 'Dey wouldn't let me leave them wit' her, but at least I
brung 'em! What did you bring? You didn't even bring your
stinkin' junkie self!

SKANK. ... Who?

CHARLIE. I woulda protected her! Kept her safe! I wouldn't a let
her be hookin' or nothin', I woulda helped her! ... I shoulda helped
her! I shoulda! ... I — *(Charlie puts on his Darth Vader mask and
takes out a knife.)* I'm crossin' to another place. I'm crossin' it, and I'm
takin' you wit' me. You didn't deserve her ... You never deserved her!
She was a princess! She was a Princess fuckin' Leia, thass who she
was! ... She was, she was ... *(Charlie takes off the mask, drops the
knife.)* I woulda made her a princess. An Arabian princess ... She
woulda ... She, she woulda ... *(Charlie empties his money out of his
pocket, a few coins and loose singles. He drops it near Skank's hands.
Charlie exits. Skank is giggling and gurgling, oblivious.)*

Scene 3

*Dawn. A park bench near the West Side highway. Skank is
drinking his hot chocolate. A beat. Lenny runs by with a
purse.*

LENNY. You seen Five-O?

SKANK. Huh?

LENNY. Cops. You seen cops?

SKANK. Nah, man.

LENNY. I know you?

SKANK. What?

56

LENNY. I know you, right? Gimme your hat.

SKANK. Hey, man. I'm juss sittin' here.

LENNY. Gimme the hat.

SKANK. Here, man.

LENNY. Switch jackets wit' me!

SKANK. What're ya talkin bout, "Jackets"?

LENNY. I got no time here, okay? Switch jackets.

SKANK. I don' think my jacket's gonna fit you, man, no offense.

LENNY. C'mon quick!

SKANK. Okay, okay ... hey, this is a nice jacket man, thanks.

LENNY. It's temporary, don't stink it up. Take this purse, hide it in your pants.

SKANK. Look, man, I'm holding here, I'm not lookin' to get busted, this is my quiet time here, bro.

LENNY. Juss hide it!

SKANK. Where I'm going to put it?

LENNY. Look man, put it in your ass, I don' care. Make it disappear.

SKANK. You should calm down, man.

LENNY. Don' tell me —

SKANK. — Here, bro, have a sip a this.

LENNY. Juss talk to me like you know me, like we been here for hours.

SKANK. Have a sip, man. Go ahead. Here, take the comics, pretend you can read.

LENNY. I could read. *(Lenny takes a sip.)* This shit is good, what is it?

SKANK. It's good, right?

LENNY. Damn, this shit is good.

SKANK. I'm gonna get that shit copyrighted, make a million dollars!

LENNY. You should.

SKANK. Hey, don't drink it all, save me some.

LENNY. Juss a little more.

SKANK. Okay ... We could share it.

LENNY. You made this shit?

SKANK. Yup.

LENNY. It's very creamy.

SKANK. I know.

LENNY. But it has a kick.

SKANK. I'm a creative person, I got skills like that.

LENNY. You see cops?

SKANK. Nah … What'd you do, knock over a ol' lady?

LENNY. She wasn't that old. She was big.

SKANK. Yeah?

LENNY. Bigger than me. She punched me.

SKANK. Yeah?

LENNY. Yeah. I was gonna punch her back, but, then I woulda felt guilty.

SKANK. How much money she got?

LENNY. I don' know. I juss ran.

SKANK. Wanna open it?

LENNY. Hey! Chill!

SKANK. I'm chill, man.

LENNY. I'm gonna take that money, buy my girl a steak dinner, shut her ass up! If I got anything left, I'm gonna get a gun, a big fuckin Gat, so motherfuckahs know I ain't playin'.

SKANK. Good idea.

LENNY. Yeah. *(Pause.)*

SKANK. Hey, you heard about Sammy?

LENNY. Sammy?

SKANK. The old guy, Sammy?

LENNY. What about him?

SKANK. He died in the bar last night.

LENNY. Really?

SKANK. When he died, Jake and the bartender, they put him on the street, laid him out like a strip a bacon, man, before they called 911. They didn't want the cops fuckin' up business, plus, something about insurance.

LENNY. Thass fucked up. *(Pause.)*

SKANK. When I die man, I wanna die here, with the sound of the traffic on the highway puttin' me to sleep.

LENNY. Yeah?

SKANK. I almost died here last week, but Chickie came by, woke me up.

LENNY. Chickie's your girl?

SKANK. Yeah ... I should go find her. She's, like, missing.

LENNY. So's mine.

SKANK. Who? Your girl?

LENNY. I don' wanna talk about it. *(Pause.)*

SKANK. A guy jerked off on my face the other night for twenty dollars, man. He came right in my eyes.

LENNY. Yeah?

SKANK. Like I was nothin'.

LENNY. Yeah.

SKANK. Twenty bucks.

LENNY. Thass okay ... At least you got twenty bucks, man.

SKANK. Thass what I'm tryin' to tell myself. *(Pause.)*

LENNY. Let's open this bag, man.

SKANK. ... Want me to go?

LENNY. ... Why? You wanna go?

SKANK. Nah, but, uh, if you want —

LENNY. Nah, man, stay ... Stay ... You can stay.

End of Play

NEW PLAYS

★ **MONTHS ON END by Craig Pospisil.** In comic scenes, one for each month of the year, we follow the intertwined worlds of a circle of friends and family whose lives are poised between happiness and heartbreak. "...a triumph...these twelve vignettes all form crucial pieces in the eternal puzzle known as human relationships, an area in which the playwright displays an assured knowledge that spans deep sorrow to unbounded happiness." –*Ann Arbor News.* "...rings with emotional truth, humor...[an] endearing contemplation on love...entertaining and satisfying." –*Oakland Press.* [5M, 5W] ISBN: 0-8222-1892-5

★ **GOOD THING by Jessica Goldberg.** Brings us into the households of John and Nancy Roy, forty-something high-school guidance counselors whose marriage has been increasingly on the rocks and Dean and Mary, recent graduates struggling to make their way in life. "...a blend of gritty social drama, poetic humor and unsubtle existential contemplation..." –*Variety.* [3M, 3W] ISBN: 0-8222-1869-0

★ **THE DEAD EYE BOY by Angus MacLachlan.** Having fallen in love at their Narcotics Anonymous meeting, Billy and Shirley-Diane are striving to overcome the past together. But their relationship is complicated by the presence of Sorin, Shirley-Diane's fourteen-year-old son, a damaged reminder of her dark past. "...a grim, insightful portrait of an unmoored family..." –*NY Times.* "MacLachlan's play isn't for the squeamish, but then, tragic stories delivered at such an unrelenting fever pitch rarely are." –*Variety.* [1M, 1W, 1 boy] ISBN: 0-8222-1844-5

★ **[SIC] by Melissa James Gibson.** In adjacent apartments three young, ambitious neighbors come together to discuss, flirt, argue, share their dreams and plan their futures with unequal degrees of deep hopefulness and abject despair. "A work...concerned with the sound and power of language..." –*NY Times.* "...a wonderfully original take on urban friendship and the comedy of manners—a *Design for Living* for our times..." –*NY Observer.* [3M, 2W] ISBN: 0-8222-1872-0

★ **LOOKING FOR NORMAL by Jane Anderson.** Roy and Irma's twenty-five-year marriage is thrown into turmoil when Roy confesses that he is actually a woman trapped in a man's body, forcing the couple to wrestle with the meaning of their marriage and the delicate dynamics of family. "Jane Anderson's bittersweet transgender domestic comedy-drama ...is thoughtful and touching and full of wit and wisdom. A real audience pleaser." –*Hollywood Reporter.* [5M, 4W] ISBN: 0-8222-1857-7

★ **ENDPAPERS by Thomas McCormack.** The regal Joshua Maynard, the old and ailing head of a mid-sized, family-owned book-publishing house in New York City, must name a successor. One faction in the house backs a smart, "pragmatic" manager, the other faction a smart, "sensitive" editor and both factions fear what the other's man could do to this house— and to them. "If Kaufman and Hart had undertaken a comedy about the publishing business, they might have written *Endpapers*...a breathlessly fast, funny, and thoughtful comedy ...keeps you amused, guessing, and often surprised...profound in its empathy for the paradoxes of human nature." –*NY Magazine.* [7M, 4W] ISBN: 0-8222-1908-5

★ **THE PAVILION by Craig Wright.** By turns poetic and comic, romantic and philosophical, this play asks old lovers to face the consequences of difficult choices made long ago. "The script's greatest strength lies in the genuineness of its feeling." –*Houston Chronicle.* "Wright's perceptive, gently witty writing makes this familiar situation fresh and thoroughly involving." –*Philadelphia Inquirer.* [2M, 1W (flexible casting)] ISBN: 0-8222-1898-4

DRAMATISTS PLAY SERVICE, INC.
440 Park Avenue South, New York, NY 10016 212-683-8960 Fax 212-213-1539
postmaster@dramatists.com www.dramatists.com

NEW PLAYS

★ **BE AGGRESSIVE by Annie Weisman.** Vista Del Sol is paradise, sandy beaches, avocado-lined streets. But for seventeen-year-old cheerleader Laura, everything changes when her mother is killed in a car crash, and she embarks on a journey to the Spirit Institute of the South where she can learn "cheer" with Bible belt intensity. "...filled with lingual gymnastics...stylized rapid-fire dialogue..." –*Variety*. "...a new, exciting, and unique voice in the American theatre..." –*BackStage West*. [1M, 4W, extras] ISBN: 0-8222-1894-1

★ **FOUR by Christopher Shinn.** Four people struggle desperately to connect in this quiet, sophisticated, moving drama. "...smart, broken-hearted...Mr. Shinn has a precocious and forgiving sense of how power shifts in the game of sexual pursuit...He promises to be a playwright to reckon with..." –*NY Times*. "A voice emerges from an American place. It's got humor, sadness and a fresh and touching rhythm that tell of the loneliness and secrets of life...[a] poetic, haunting play." –*NY Post*. [3M, 1W] ISBN: 0-8222-1850-X

★ **WONDER OF THE WORLD by David Lindsay-Abaire.** A madcap picaresque involving Niagara Falls, a lonely tour-boat captain, a pair of bickering private detectives and a husband's dirty little secret. "Exceedingly whimsical and playfully wicked. Winning and genial. A top-drawer production." –*NY Times*. "Full frontal lunacy is on display. A most assuredly fresh and hilarious tragicomedy of marital discord run amok...absolutely hysterical..." –*Variety*. [3M, 4W (doubling)] ISBN: 0-8222-1863-1

★ **QED by Peter Parnell.** Nobel Prize-winning physicist and all-around genius Richard Feynman holds forth with captivating wit and wisdom in this fascinating biographical play that originally starred Alan Alda. "QED is a seductive mix of science, human affections, moral courage, and comic eccentricity. It reflects on, among other things, death, the absence of God, travel to an unexplored country, the pleasures of drumming, and the need to know and understand." –*NY Magazine*. "Its rhythms correspond to the way that people—even geniuses—approach and avoid highly emotional issues, and it portrays Feynman with affection and awe." –*The New Yorker*. [1M, 1W] ISBN: 0-8222-1924-7

★ **UNWRAP YOUR CANDY by Doug Wright.** Alternately chilling and hilarious, this deliciously macabre collection of four bedtime tales for adults is guaranteed to keep you awake for nights on end. "Engaging and intellectually satisfying...a treat to watch." –*NY Times*. "Fiendishly clever. Mordantly funny and chilling. Doug Wright teases, freezes and zaps us." –*Village Voice*. "Four bite-size plays that bite back." –*Variety*. [flexible casting] ISBN: 0-8222-1871-2

★ **FURTHER THAN THE FURTHEST THING by Zinnie Harris.** On a remote island in the middle of the Atlantic secrets are buried. When the outside world comes calling, the islanders find their world blown apart from the inside as well as beyond. "Harris winningly produces an intimate and poetic, as well as political, family saga." –*Independent (London)*. "Harris' enthralling adventure of a play marks a departure from stale, well-furrowed theatrical terrain." –*Evening Standard (London)*. [3M, 2W] ISBN: 0-8222-1874-7

★ **THE DESIGNATED MOURNER by Wallace Shawn.** The story of three people living in a country where what sort of books people like to read and how they choose to amuse themselves becomes both firmly personal and unexpectedly entangled with questions of survival. "This is a playwright who does not just tell you what it is like to be arrested at night by goons or to fall morally apart and become an aimless yet weirdly contented ghost yourself. He has the originality to make you feel it." –*Times (London)*. "A fascinating play with beautiful passages of writing..." –*Variety*. [2M, 1W] ISBN: 0-8222-1848-8

DRAMATISTS PLAY SERVICE, INC.
440 Park Avenue South, New York, NY 10016 212-683-8960 Fax 212-213-1539
postmaster@dramatists.com   www.dramatists.com

NEW PLAYS

★ **SHEL'S SHORTS by Shel Silverstein.** Lauded poet, songwriter and author of children's books, the incomparable Shel Silverstein's short plays are deeply infused with the same wicked sense of humor that made him famous. "…[a] childlike honesty and twisted sense of humor." *–Boston Herald.* "…terse dialogue and an absurdity laced with a tang of dread give [*Shel's Shorts*] more than a trace of Samuel Beckett's comic existentialism." *–Boston Phoenix.* [flexible casting] ISBN: 0-8222-1897-6

★ **AN ADULT EVENING OF SHEL SILVERSTEIN by Shel Silverstein.** Welcome to the darkly comic world of Shel Silverstein, a world where nothing is as it seems and where the most innocent conversation can turn menacing in an instant. These ten imaginative plays vary widely in content, but the style is unmistakable. "…[*An Adult Evening*] shows off Silverstein's virtuosic gift for wordplay…[and] sends the audience out…with a clear appreciation of human nature as perverse and laughable." *–NY Times.* [flexible casting] ISBN: 0-8222-1873-9

★ **WHERE'S MY MONEY? by John Patrick Shanley.** A caustic and sardonic vivisection of the institution of marriage, laced with the author's inimitable razor-sharp wit. "…Shanley's gift for acid-laced one-liners and emotionally tumescent exchanges is certainly potent…" *–Variety.* "…lively, smart, occasionally scary and rich in reverse wisdom." *–NY Times.* [3M, 3W] ISBN: 0-8222-1865-8

★ **A FEW STOUT INDIVIDUALS by John Guare.** A wonderfully screwy comedy-drama that figures Ulysses S. Grant in the throes of writing his memoirs, surrounded by a cast of fantastical characters, including the Emperor and Empress of Japan, the opera star Adelina Patti and Mark Twain. "Guare's smarts, passion and creativity skyrocket to awesome heights…" *–Star Ledger.* "…precisely the kind of good new play that you might call an everyday miracle…every minute of it is fresh and newly alive…" *–Village Voice.* [10M, 3W] ISBN: 0-8222-1907-7

★ **BREATH, BOOM by Kia Corthron.** A look at fourteen years in the life of Prix, a Bronx native, from her ruthless girl-gang leadership at sixteen through her coming to maturity at thirty. "…vivid world, believable and eye-opening, a place worthy of a dramatic visit, where no one would want to live but many have to." *–NY Times.* "…rich with humor, terse vernacular strength and gritty detail…" *–Variety.* [1M, 9W] ISBN: 0-8222-1849-6

★ **THE LATE HENRY MOSS by Sam Shepard.** Two antagonistic brothers, Ray and Earl, are brought together after their father, Henry Moss, is found dead in his seedy New Mexico home in this classic Shepard tale. "…His singular gift has been for building mysteries out of the ordinary ingredients of American family life…" *–NY Times.* "…rich moments …Shepard finds gold." *–LA Times.* [7M, 1W] ISBN: 0-8222-1858-5

★ **THE CARPETBAGGER'S CHILDREN by Horton Foote.** One family's history spanning from the Civil War to WWII is recounted by three sisters in evocative, intertwining monologues. "…bittersweet music—[a] rhapsody of ambivalence…in its modest, garrulous way…theatrically daring." *–The New Yorker.* [3W] ISBN: 0-8222-1843-7

★ **THE NINA VARIATIONS by Steven Dietz.** In this funny, fierce and heartbreaking homage to *The Seagull*, Dietz puts Chekhov's star-crossed lovers in a room and doesn't let them out. "A perfect little jewel of a play…" *–Shepherdstown Chronicle.* "…a delightful revelation of a writer at play; and also an odd, haunting, moving theater piece of lingering beauty." *–Eastside Journal (Seattle).* [1M, 1W (flexible casting)] ISBN: 0-8222-1891-7

DRAMATISTS PLAY SERVICE, INC.
440 Park Avenue South, New York, NY 10016 212-683-8960 Fax 212-213-1539
postmaster@dramatists.com www.dramatists.com